PLANET URANUS

By Rosie Rowntree

CONTENTS

First published in 2026 by Hungry Tomato Ltd
F15, Old Bakery Studios, Blewetts Wharf, Malpas Road,
Truro, Cornwall, TR1 1QH, UK.

A CIP catalog record for this book is available from the British Library.

ISBN 9781835696828

Manufactured in the USA

Discover more at
www.hungrytomato.com

Front cover image is an artist's impression of Uranus as seen from the surface of one of its moons. Title page image is an edited image of Uranus. Contents page image is an edited image of Uranus and its rings.

Words in **BOLD** can be found in the glossary.

WHERE IS URANUS?

There are eight planets in our **solar system**. The planets travel around the Sun. Uranus is the seventh planet from the Sun.

The time it takes a planet to travel around the Sun is called a year. Uranus travels around the Sun once every 84 **Earth years**. This journey is called an **orbit**.

PLANET FACTS

Uranus is one of two "ice giants" in our solar system, alongside Neptune.

Ice giants like Uranus don't have a solid surface. They are instead made of a thick mixture of water and two **gases** called **methane** and **ammonia**. It is this methane gas that makes Uranus look blue.

Uranus is tilted on its side and spins in a completely different way to the other planets. Scientists think it was hit by something the size of Earth billions of years ago. The impact was so big that it knocked Uranus over!

A day is the time it takes a planet to spin around once. A day on Uranus is the same as 17 ½ hours on Earth.

WHAT'S THE WEATHER LIKE?

As its "ice giant" title suggests, Uranus is a very cold planet. It is the coldest in the solar system!

When the methane in Uranus's atmosphere is squeezed under **pressure**, tiny diamonds can be formed. Some scientists think that it might rain diamonds on Uranus!

Diamond rain!

Temperatures in Uranus's **atmosphere** are as low as -371 °F (-224 °C)! The lowest temperature ever reached on Earth is -128 °F (-89 °C).

URANUS'S MOONS

Uranus has 28 **moons** that scientists know of. The five largest are named after characters from plays of the famous writer, William Shakespeare!

Miranda is a very strange-looking moon, covered in cliffs, valleys, and **craters**. Due to Uranus's low **gravity**, if a rock was dropped off the top of the tallest cliff it would take ten minutes to reach the bottom!

It has a huge canyon running for almost 932 miles (1,500 kilometers)! Scientists think it was created by Titania freezing and expanding.

URANUS'S RINGS

As well as its moons, Uranus has several faint, narrow rings surrounding it.

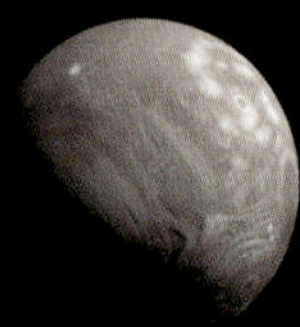

The moon Miranda

Where Saturn's rings are bright and easy to see even with small telescopes, Uranus's rings are much harder to spot. In fact, they were discovered over 350 years later than Saturn's!

Scientists think that they were created by several of Uranus's moons crashing into each other billions of years ago.

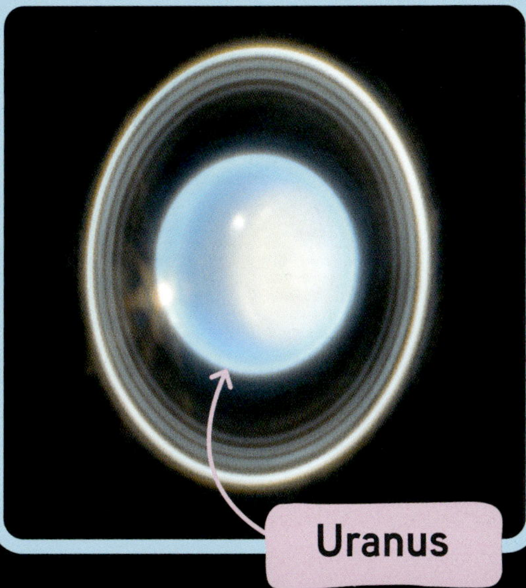

This image was taken by the **James Webb Space Telescope**. It used special filters to make Uranus and its rings seem brighter than they are.

SEASONS ON URANUS

Just like Earth, Uranus has four **seasons**. But Uranus's are a lot longer and far more extreme!

Because of the unusual angle that Uranus tilts at, one of the planet's **poles** faces the Sun in a summer that lasts for 21 years! This puts the other pole into a pitch-black winter that also lasts for 21 years.

When the dark areas of the planet finally emerge from their winter, it causes huge storms the size of whole countries!

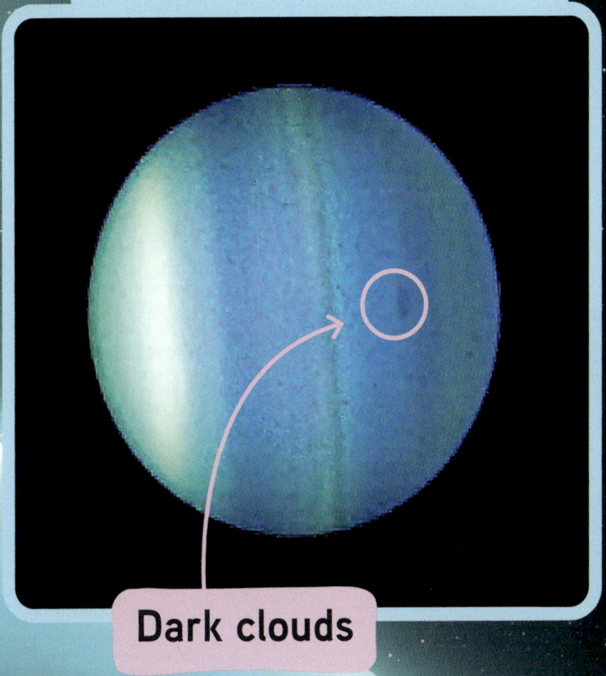

FACT FILE

Because of its distance from Earth, a lot about Uranus is still a mystery. But there are some things that we know for sure.

Uranus is the third largest planet in the solar system, behind Jupiter and Saturn. It is four times as wide as Earth!

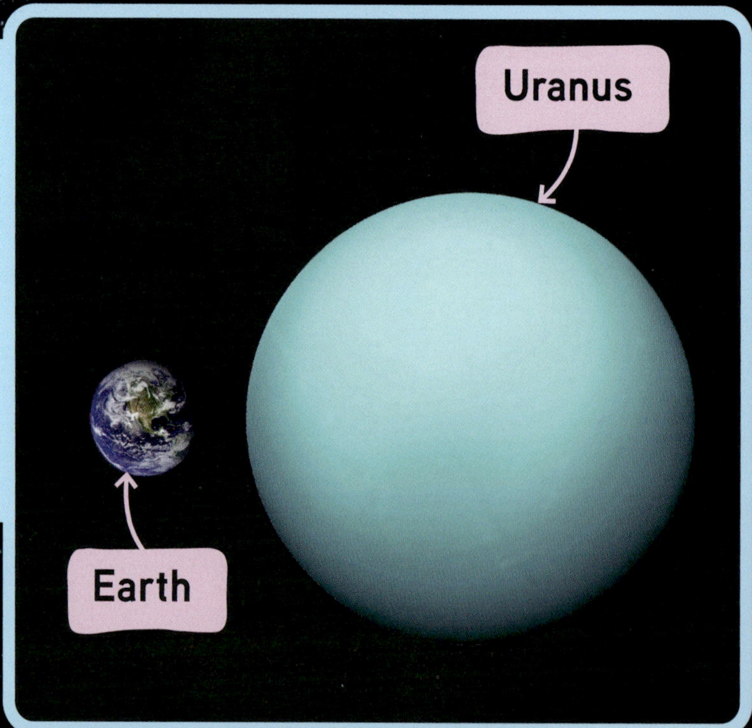

Uranus is the only planet named after a Greek god instead of a Roman god. It was named after the Greek god of the sky. But its original name was "George", after the King of England at the time of the planet's discovery!

WHAT CAN WE SEE?

Studying Uranus from Earth is difficult because it is so far away. It is barely visible with the human eye at night and looks like a very distant star.

Telescope

Viewing Uranus from Earth is best done with a **telescope**. In fact, it was the first planet ever discovered using a telescope!

Space telescope

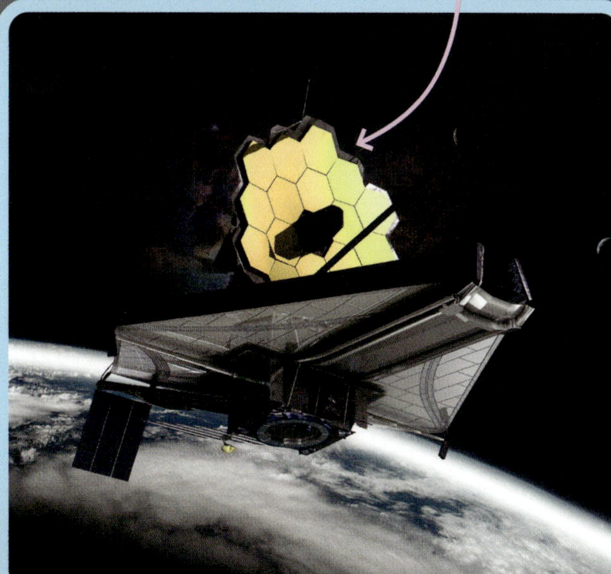

The best photographs of Uranus come from **space telescopes** in orbit around Earth. Because they are outside Earth's atmosphere, the images these telescopes create are a lot clearer.

EXPLORING URANUS

Only one spacecraft has ever visited Uranus! Voyager 2 made plenty of discoveries about this distant planet.

It is thanks to this spacecraft that scientists discovered Uranus's unusual tilt, as well as many of its moons.

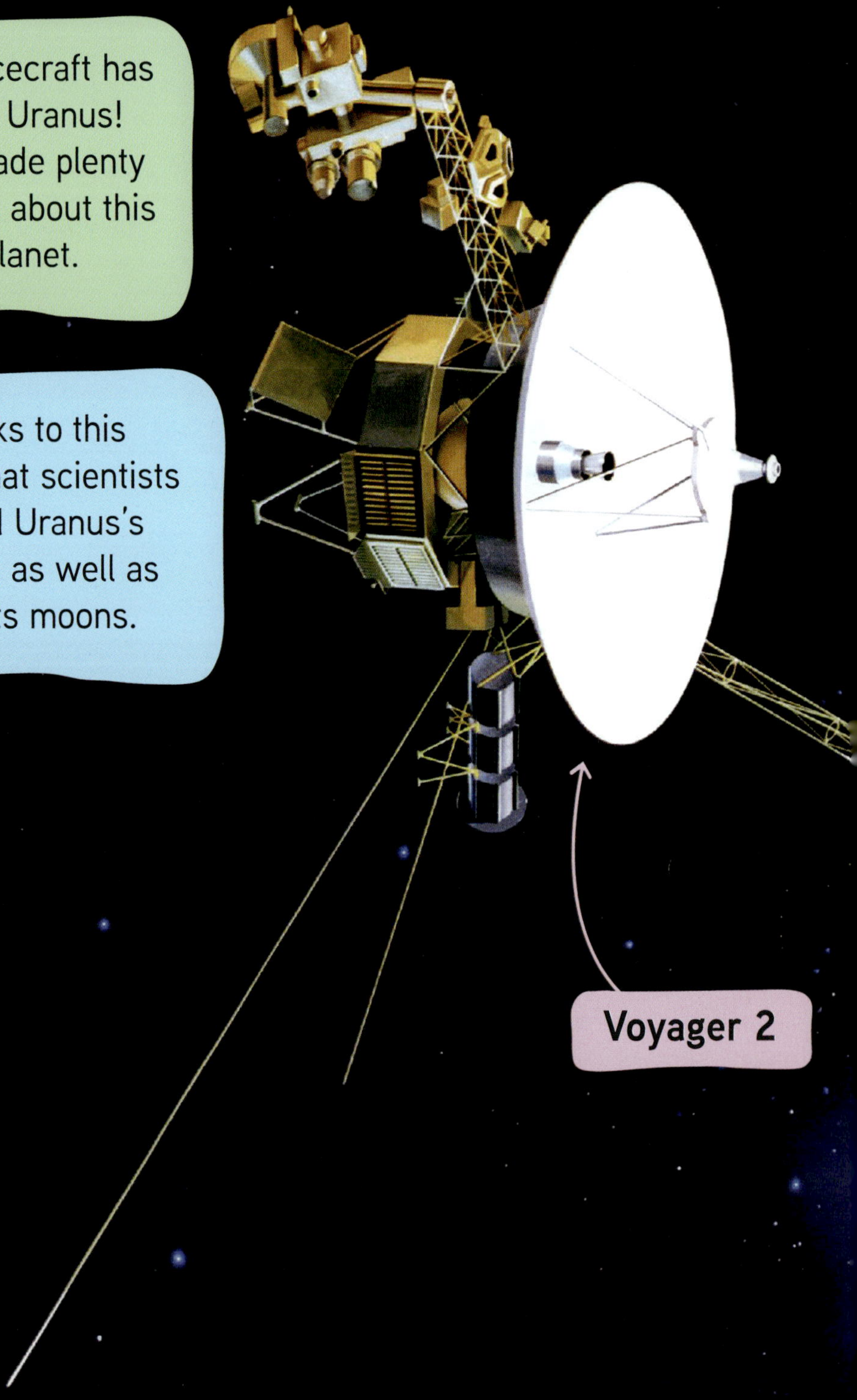

Voyager 2 launched in 1977 and took nine years to reach Uranus!

Voyager 2 didn't stop at Uranus – it kept going! It flew past Neptune and is now in **interstellar space**.

WHAT'S NEXT?

Since only one spacecraft has visited Uranus, there is still a lot that scientists are keen to learn about the planet.

New missions are planning to go back to Uranus to explore more!

Voyager 2's visit to Uranus might have happened at the same time as a powerful **solar storm**. This storm could have hidden key details about Uranus and its moons.

Scientists now believe that some of Uranus's moons could have oceans beneath their surfaces. Water is very important for life!

GLOSSARY

Ammonia – a colorless gas.

Atmosphere – the gases that surround a planet.

Craters – large holes that have been created by something hitting the ground.

Earth years – the amount of time that a year lasts for on Earth (365 days).

Interstellar space – the space between stars.

James Webb Space Telescope – a telescope in orbit around Earth.

Gases – substances that are neither solid or liquid and have no fixed shape. Many gases are invisible.

Gravity – an invisible force that pulls things together. Gravity keeps our feet on the ground and the planets spinning around the Sun.

Methane – a tasteless gas.

Moons – large, natural objects that orbit a planet.

Orbit – the path taken by one object circling around another object in space.

Poles – the points furthest north and south on a planet.

Pressure – a force that pushes on something.

Seasons – different times of the year, with different types of weather. Spring, summer, fall, and winter are all seasons.

Solar storm – an explosion of energy from the Sun.

Solar system – the Sun and everything that moves around it.

Space telescopes – telescopes in orbit in space.

Telescope – an instrument that makes faraway objects appear bigger.

Picture credits:
(t=top; b=bottom; m=middle; l=left; r=right):

NASA: images-assets.nasa.gov/image/PIA01490/PIA01490~orig.jpg 10br; images-assets.nasa.gov/image/PIA04495/PIA04495~orig.jpg 20-21bg; images-assets.nasa.gov/image/PIA21744/PIA21744~orig.jpg 21tr; images-assets.nasa.gov/image/PIA17306/PIA17306~-orig.jpg 14m. Wikipedia: By Johann Zoffany - Royal Collection RCIN 405072, Public Domain 17br; By NASA Hubble - https://www.flickr.com/photos/144614754@N02/46455057294/, CC BY 2.0 15mr; By NASA, ESA, CSA, STScI, J. DePasquale (STScI), CC BY 4.0 13tl; By Orange-kun (old version user: Brian0918) - This image was made from NASA Earth America 2010.jpg and Uranus2.jpg (colour adjustment) or Uranus (Edited).jpg, Public Domain 16br. Unknown 11m. Shutterstock: AstroStar 19tl; Beyond Space 7mr; Buradaki 6-7bg, 8-7bg; Fer Gregory 8bl; gidenilson 4-5bg; Janez Volmajer 14-15bg; Jdmkci 2-3bg; Manumata 12-13bg, 22-23bg; Media Whale Stock 16-17bg; Mike Mareen 18-19bg; NASA Images 1bg; PaoPano 19br; Remotevfx.com 22br; Vadim Sadovski 10-11bg, 24bg.